1

"Be yourself; everyone else is
already taken."
— Oscar Wilde

2

"Be the change that you wish to
see in the world."
— Mahatma Gandhi

3

"Live as if you were to die
tomorrow. Learn as if you were
to live forever."
— Mahatma Gandhi

4
"Without music, life would be a mistake."
— Friedrich Nietzsche

5
"We accept the love we think we deserve."
— Stephen Chbosky

6
"Imperfection is beauty, madness is genius and it's better to be absolutely ridiculous than absolutely boring."
— Marilyn Monroe

7
"Yesterday is history, tomorrow is a mystery, today is a gift of God, which is why we call it the present."
— Bil Keane

8
"We are all in the gutter, but some of us are looking at the stars."
— Oscar Wilde

9
"I have not failed. I've just found 10,000 ways that won't work."
— Thomas A. Edison

10

"Fairy tales are more than true: not because they tell us that dragons exist, but because they tell us that dragons can be beaten."
— Neil Gaiman

11

"It is never too late to be what you might have been."
— George Eliot

12

"There is no greater agony than bearing an untold story inside you."
— Maya Angelou

13

"Everything you can imagine
is real."
— Pablo Picasso

14

"You can never get a cup of tea
large enough or a book long
enough to suit me."
— C.S. Lewis

15

"To the well-organized mind,
death is but the next great
adventure."
— J.K. Rowling

16

"Do what you can, with what you have, where you are."
— Theodore Roosevelt

17

"Life isn't about finding yourself.
Life is about creating yourself."
— George Bernard Shaw

18

"Success is not final, failure is not fatal: it is the courage to continue that counts."
— Winston S. Churchill

19

"Do one thing every day that scares you."
— Eleanor Roosevelt

20

"So, this is my life. And I want you to know that I am both happy and sad and I'm still trying to figure out how that could be."
— Stephen Chbosky

21

"You may say I'm a dreamer, but I'm not the only one. I hope someday you'll join us. And the world will live as one."
— John Lennon

22

"We believe in ordinary acts of bravery, in the courage that drives one person to stand up for another."
— Veronica Roth

23

"And, when you want something, all the universe conspires in helping you to achieve it."
— Paulo Coelho

24

"It's no use going back to yesterday, because I was a different person then."
— Lewis Carroll

25

"We are what we pretend to be, so we must be careful about what we pretend to be."
— Kurt Vonnegut

26

"A person's a person, no matter how small."
— Dr. Seuss

27

"It's the possibility of having a dream come true that makes life interesting."
— Paulo Coelho

28

"You can't live your life for other people. You've got to do what's right for you, even if it hurts some people you love."
— Nicholas Sparks

29

"Well-behaved women seldom make history."
— Laurel Thatcher Ulrich

30

"Nothing is impossible, the word itself says 'I'm possible'!"
— Audrey Hepburn

34
"Peace begins with a smile.."
— Mother Teresa

35
"When we love, we always strive to become better than we are. When we strive to become better than we are, everything around us becomes better too."
— Paulo Coelho

36
"Sometimes you wake up. Sometimes the fall kills you. And sometimes, when you fall, you fly."
— Neil Gaiman

31

"I can't give you a sure-fire formula for success, but I can give you a formula for failure: try to please everybody all the time."
— Herbert Bayard Swope

32

"Do what you feel in your heart to be right – for you'll be criticized anyway."
— Eleanor Roosevelt

33

"Happiness is not something ready made. It comes from your own actions."
— Dalai Lama XIV

37
"Don't think or judge, just listen."
— Sarah Dessen

38

"So we beat on, boats against the current, borne back ceaselessly into the past."
— F. Scott Fitzgerald

39
"Do not read, as children do, to amuse yourself, or like the ambitious, for the purpose of instruction. No, read in order to live."
— Gustave Flaubert

40

"What lies behind us and what lies before us are tiny matters compared to what lies within us."
— Ralph Waldo Emerson

41

"Never doubt that a small group of thoughtful, committed, citizens can change the world. Indeed, it is the only thing that ever has."
— Margaret Mead

42

"First they ignore you, then they ridicule you, then they fight you, and then you win."
— Mahatma Gandhi

43
"Hold fast to dreams,
For if dreams die
Life is a broken-winged bird,
That cannot fly."
— Langston Hughes

44
"Two wrongs don't make a right,
but they make a good excuse."
— Thomas Szasz

45
"Whatever you are, be a good
one."
— Abraham Lincoln

46

"Friendship is unnecessary, like philosophy, like art.... It has no survival value; rather it is one of those things which give value to survival."
— C.S. Lewis

47

"I hope she'll be a fool -- that's the best thing a girl can be in this world, a beautiful little fool."
— F. Scott Fitzgerald

48

"May you live every day of your life."
— Jonathan Swift

49
"You can't stay in your corner of the Forest waiting for others to come to you. You have to go to them sometimes."
— A.A. Milne

50
"Isn't it nice to think that tomorrow is a new day with no mistakes in it yet?"
— L.M. Montgomery

51
"If my life is going to mean anything, I have to live it myself."
— Rick Riordan

52

"I have no special talents. I am only passionately curious."
— Albert Einstein

53

"What's meant to be will always find a way"
— Trisha Yearwood

54

"Always do what you are afraid to do."
— Ralph Waldo Emerson

55

"Faith is taking the first step even when you can't see the whole staircase."
— Martin Luther King Jr.

56

"Hope is the thing with feathers
That perches in the soul
And sings the tune without the words
And never stops at all."
— Emily Dickinson

57

"Our lives begin to end the day we become silent about things that matter."
— Martin Luther King Jr.

58

"Your task is not to seek for love, but merely to seek and find all the barriers within yourself that you have built against it."
— Jalaluddin Rumi

59

"In the end, we will remember not the words of our enemies, but the silence of our friends."
— Martin Luther King Jr.

60

"It is so hard to leave—until you leave. And then it is the easiest goddamned thing in the world."
— John Green

61

"The flower that blooms in adversity is the rarest and most beautiful of all."
— Walt Disney Company

62

"Talent hits a target no one else can hit. Genius hits a target no one else can see."
— Arthur Schopenhauer

63

"If you're reading this...
Congratulations, you're alive.
If that's not something to smile about,
then I don't know what is."
— Chad Sugg

67

"When you have eliminated all which is impossible, then whatever remains, however improbable, must be the truth."
— Arthur Conan Doyle

68

"Turn your wounds into wisdom."
— Oprah Winfrey

69

"Never let your sense of morals prevent you from doing what is right."
— Isaac Asimov

64

"He who controls the past controls the future. He who controls the present controls the past."

— George Orwell

65

"The mind is its own place, and in itself can make a heaven of hell, a hell of heaven.."

— John Milton

66

"We delight in the beauty of the butterfly, but rarely admit the changes it has gone through to achieve that beauty."

— Maya Angelou

70

"Waiting is painful. Forgetting is painful. But not knowing which to do is the worst kind of suffering."
— Paulo Coelho

71

"Fantasy is hardly an escape from reality. It's a way of understanding it."
— Lloyd Alexander

72

"Do not go where the path may lead, go instead where there is no path and leave a trail."
— Ralph Waldo Emerson

73

"You never have to change anything you got up in the middle of the night to write."
— Saul Bellow

74

"If you can't fly then run, if you can't run then walk, if you can't walk then crawl, but whatever you do you have to keep moving forward."
— Martin Luther King Jr.

75

"I love to see a young girl go out and grab the world by the lapels. Life's a bitch. You've got to go out and kick ass."
— Maya Angelou

76

"And, in the end
The love you take
is equal to the love you make."
— Paul McCartney

77

"The unexamined life is not
worth living."
— Socrates

78

"What I need is the dandelion in
the spring. The bright yellow
that means rebirth instead of
destruction. The promise that
life can go on, no matter how
bad our losses. That it can be
good again."
— Suzanne Collins

79

"Courage is the most important of all the virtues because without courage, you can't practice any other virtue consistently."
— Maya Angelou

80

"Hell is empty and all the devils are here."
— William Shakespeare

81

"The future belongs to those who believe in the beauty of their dreams."
— Eleanor Roosevelt

82

"Prayer is not asking. It is a longing of the soul. It is daily admission of one's weakness. It is better in prayer to have a heart without words than words without a heart."

— Mahatma Gandhi

83

"One day, in retrospect, the years of struggle will strike you as the most beautiful."

— Sigmund Freud

84

"None but ourselves can free our minds."

— Bob Marley

85

"I don't trust people who don't love themselves and tell me, 'I love you.' ... There is an African saying which is: Be careful when a naked person offers you a shirt."
— Maya Angelou

86

"War is peace.
Freedom is slavery.
Ignorance is strength."
— George Orwell (1984)

87

"Don't judge each day by the harvest you reap but by the seeds that you plant."
— Robert Louis Stevenson

88

"If you remember me, then I
don't care if everyone else
forgets."
— Haruki Murakami

89

"Sometimes our light goes out,
but is blown again into instant
flame by an encounter with
another human being."
— Albert Schweitzer

90

"I was never really insane
except upon occasions when my
heart was touched."
— Edgar Allan Poe

91

"Only in the darkness can you
see the stars."
— Martin Luther King Jr.

92

"A woman's heart should be so
hidden in God that a man has to
seek Him just to find her."
— Max Lucado

93

"It's kind of fun to do the
impossible."
— Walt Disney Company

94

"Let no man pull you so low as to hate him."
— Martin Luther King Jr.

95

"I do not fear death. I had been dead for billions and billions of years before I was born, and had not suffered the slightest inconvenience from it."
— Mark Twain

96

"A painter should begin every canvas with a wash of black, because all things in nature are dark except where exposed by the light."
— Leonardo da Vinci

97

"Pain is temporary. Quitting lasts forever."
— Lance Armstrong

98

"The Chinese use two brush strokes to write the word 'crisis.' One brush stroke stands for danger; the other for opportunity. In a crisis, be aware of the danger--but recognize the opportunity."
— John F. Kennedy

99

"It's not the load that breaks you down, it's the way you carry it."
— Lou Holtz

100

"I was smiling yesterday,I am smiling today and I will smile tomorrow.Simply because life is too short to cry for anything."
— Santosh Kalwar

101

"It's not the load that breaks you down, it's the way you carry it."
— Lou Holtz

102

"The things you do for yourself are gone when you are gone, but the things you do for others remain as your legacy."
— Kalu Ndukwe Kalu

103

"All the darkness in the world cannot extinguish the light of a single candle."
— Francis of Assisi

104

"You never fail until you stop trying."
— Albert Einstein

105

"You're off to Great Places!
Today is your day!
Your mountain is waiting,
So... get on your way!"
— Dr. Seuss

106

"Why didn't I learn to treat everything like it was the last time. My greatest regret was how much I believed in the future."
— Jonathan Safran Foer

107

"Hope
Smiles from the threshold of the year to come,
Whispering 'it will be happier'..."
— Alfred Tennyson

108

"One love, one heart, one destiny."
— Bob Marley

109

"Don't be afraid of your fears. They're not there to scare you. They're there to let you know that something is worth it."
— C. Joy Bell C.

110

"Is 'fat' really the worst thing a human being can be? Is 'fat' worse than 'vindictive', 'jealous', 'shallow', 'vain', 'boring' or 'cruel'? Not to me."
— J.K. Rowling

111

"Once you have tasted flight, you will forever walk the earth with your eyes turned skyward, for there you have been, and there you will always long to return."
— Leonardo da Vinci

112

"To see a World in a Grain of Sand
And a Heaven in a Wild Flower,
Hold Infinity in the palm of your hand
And Eternity in an hour."
— William Blake

113

"So be sure when you step, Step with
care and great tact. And remember
that life's A Great Balancing Act. And
will you succeed? Yes! You will,
indeed! (98 and ¾ percent guaranteed)
Kid, you'll move mountains."
— Dr. Seuss

114

"You see things; you say, 'Why?'
But I dream things that never
were; and I say 'Why not?"
— George Bernard Shaw

115

"Clouds come floating into my life, no longer to carry rain or usher storm, but to add color to my sunset sky."
— Rabindranath Tagore

116

"If she's amazing, she won't be easy. If she's easy, she won't be amazing. If she's worth it, you wont give up. If you give up, you're not worthy. ... Truth is, everybody is going to hurt you; you just gotta find the ones worth suffering for."
— Bob Marley

117

"Live in the present, remember the past, and fear not the future, for it doesn't exist and never shall. There is only now."
— Christopher Paolini

118

"You is kind. You is smart. You is important."
— Kathryn Stockett

119

"You is kind. You is smart. You is important."
— Kathryn Stockett

120

"Any fool can be happy. It takes a man with real heart to make beauty out of the stuff that makes us weep."
— Clive Barker

121

"Start writing, no matter what.
The water does not flow until
the faucet is turned on."
— Louis L'Amour

122

"Dance, when you're broken open.
Dance, if you've torn the bandage off.
Dance in the middle of the fighting.
Dance in your blood. Dance when
you're perfectly free."
— Jalaluddin Rumi

123

"Better to be strong than pretty
and useless."
— Lilith Saintcrow

124

"If you are irritated by every rub, how will your mirror be polished?"
— Jalaluddin Rumi

125

"Better to be strong than pretty and useless."
— Lilith Saintcrow

126

"You need to learn how to select your thoughts just the same way you select your clothes every day. This is a power you can cultivate. If you want to control things in your life so bad, work on the mind. That's the only thing you should be trying to control."
— Elizabeth Gilbert

127

"Even if you are on the right track, you'll get run over if you just sit there."
— Will Rogers

128

"Life is a shipwreck, but we must not forget to sing in the lifeboats."
— Voltaire

129

"You were born with wings, why prefer to crawl through life?"
— Jalaluddin Rumi

130

"Though nobody can go back and make a new beginning... Anyone can start over and make a new ending."
— Chico Xavier

131

"We are just an advanced breed of monkeys on a minor planet of a very average star. But we can understand the Universe. That makes us something very special."
— Stephen Hawking

132

"The most common way people give up their power is by thinking they don't have any."
— Alice Walker

133
"I dream my painting and I paint
my dream."
— Vincent Van Gogh

134
"A ship is safe in harbor, but
that's not what ships are for."
— William G.T. Shedd

135
"You should never be surprised
when someone treats you with
respect, you should expect it."
— Sarah Dessen

136

"People say nothing is impossible, but I do nothing every day."
— A.A. Milne

137

"Maybe everyone can live beyond what they're capable of."
— Markus Zusak

138

"What you do makes a difference, and you have to decide what kind of difference you want to make."
— Jane Goodall

139

"Do you want to know who you are? Don't ask. Act! Action will delineate and define you."
— Thomas Jefferson

140

"What makes the desert beautiful,' said the little prince, 'is that somewhere it hides a well...'"
— Antoine de Saint-Exupéry

141

"You will find that it is necessary to let things go; simply for the reason that they are heavy. So let them go, let go of them. I tie no weights to my ankles."
— C. JoyBell C.

145
"The worst part of success is trying to find someone who is happy for you."
— Bette Midler

146
"What's the good of living if you don't try a few things?"
— Charles M. Schulz

147
"May the forces of evil become confused on the way to your house."
— George Carlin

142

"Happiness [is] only real when shared"
— Jon Krakauer

143

"Don't be satisfied with stories, how things have gone with others. Unfold your own myth."
— Jalaluddin Rumi

144

"If you treat an individual as he is, he will remain how he is. But if you treat him as if he were what he ought to be and could be, he will become what he ought to be and could be."
— Johann Wolfgang von Goethe

148

"And in the end it is not the years in your life that count, it's the life in your years."
— Abraham Lincoln

149

"Try a little harder to be a little better."
— Gordon B. Hinckley

150

"You yourself, as much as anybody in the entire universe, deserve your love and affection"
— Sharon Salzberg

151
"Love is the absence of
judgment."
— Dalai Lama XIV

152
"There are years that ask
questions and years that answer."
— Zora Neale Hurston

153
"The past has no power over the
present moment."
— Eckhart Tolle

154

"Reputation is what other people know about you. Honor is what you know about yourself."
— Lois McMaster Bujold

155

"When people don't express themselves, they die one piece at a time."
— Laurie Halse Anderson

156

"When I was about eight, I decided that the most wonderful thing, next to a human being, was a book."
— Margaret Walker

160

"I kept always two books in my pocket, one to read, one to write in."
— Robert Louis Stevenson

161

"It's not the size of the dog in the fight, it's the size of the fight in the dog."
— Mark Twain

162

"Lack of direction, not lack of time, is the problem. We all have twenty-four hour days."
— Zig Ziglar

157

"There was another life that I might have had, but I am having this one."
— Kazuo Ishiguro

158

"Remember, darkness does not always equate to evil, just as light does not always bring good."
— P.C. Cast

159

"No matter what he does, every person on earth plays a central role in the history of the world. And normally he doesn't know it."
— Paulo Coelho

163

"I meant what I said and I said
what I meant. An elephant's
faithful one-hundred percent!"
— Dr. Seuss

164

"Nothing in the world is ever
completely wrong. Even a stopped
clock is right twice a day."
— Paulo Coelho

165

"Letting go means to come to the
realization that some people are
a part of your history, but not a
part of your destiny."
— Steve Maraboli

166

"If you think you are too small to make a difference, try sleeping with a mosquito."
— Dalai Lama XIV

167

"There must be those among whom we can sit down and weep and still be counted as warriors."
— Adrienne Rich

168

"You have power over your mind - not outside events. Realize this, and you will find strength."
— Marcus Aurelius

169

"Anyone can hide. Facing up to things, working through them, that's what makes you strong."
— Sarah Dessen

170

"The greatness of a man is not in how much wealth he acquires, but in his integrity and his ability to affect those around him positively"
— Bob Marley

171

"The glory of friendship is not the outstretched hand, not the kindly smile, nor the joy of companionship; it is the spiritual inspiration that comes to one when you discover that someone else believes in you and is willing to trust you with a friendship."
— Ralph Waldo Emerson

172

"In the end
these things matter most:
How well did you love?
How fully did you live?
How deeply did you let go?"
— Jack Kornfield

173

"Go on with what your heart tells
you, or you will lose all."
— Rick Riordan

174

"What do we live for, if it is not
to make life less difficult for
each other?"
— George Eliot

175

"The purpose of life is to live it, to taste experience to the utmost, to reach out eagerly and without fear for newer and richer experience."
— Eleanor Roosevelt

176

"Change will not come if we wait for some other person, or if we wait for some other time. We are the ones we've been waiting for. We are the change that we seek."
— Barack Obama

177

"Thinking something does not make it true. Wanting something does not make it real."
— Michelle Hodkin

178

"When one tugs at a single thing
in nature, he finds it attached to
the rest of the world."
— John Muir

179

"Kindness is a language which
the deaf can hear and the blind
can see."
— Mark Twain

180

"It is the time you have wasted
for your rose that makes your
rose so important."
— Antoine de Saint-Exupéry

181

"please believe that things are good with me, and even when they're not, they will be soon enough. And i will always believe the same about you."
— Stephen Chbosky

182

"My concern is not whether God is on our side; my greatest concern is to be on God's side, for God is always right."
— Abraham Lincoln

183

"Great heroes need great sorrows and burdens, or half their greatness goes unnoticed. It is all part of the fairy tale."
— Peter S. Beagle

184
"I'd rather be hated for who I am,
than loved for who I am not."
— Kurt Cobain

185
"A woman's heart should be so
hidden in God that a man has to
seek Him just to find her."
— Maya Angelou

186
"Trees that are slow to grow
bear the best fruit."
— Molière

187

"Tears are words that need to be
written."
— Paulo Coelho

188

"The most beautiful things in the
world cannot be seen or touched,
they are felt with the heart."
— Antoine de Saint-Exupéry

189

"Never be bullied into silence.
Never allow yourself to be made
a victim. Accept no one's
definition of your life, but define
yourself."
— Harvey Fierstein

190

"Never be bullied into silence. Never allow yourself to be made a victim. Accept no one's definition of your life, but define yourself."
— Harvey Fierstein

191

"Wanting to be someone else is a waste of the person you are."
— Marilyn Monroe

192

"It does not matter how slowly you go as long as you do not stop."
— Confucius

193

"Ignore those that make you fearful
and sad, that degrade you back
towards disease and death."
— Jalaluddin Rumi

194

"I wonder how many people don't get
the one they want, but end up with the
one they're supposed to be with."
— Fannie Flagg

195

"Parents can only give good
advice or put them on the right
paths, but the final forming of a
person's character lies in their
own hands."
— Anne Frank

196

"To give pleasure to a single heart by a single act is better than a thousand heads bowing in prayer."
— Mahatma Gandhi

197

"Even strength must bow to wisdom sometimes."
— Rick Riordan

198

"Cry. Forgive. Learn. Move on. Let your tears water the seeds of your future happiness."
— Steve Maraboli

199

"I don't think of all the misery, but of the beauty that still remains."
— Anne Frank

200

"We don't need a list of rights and wrongs, tables of dos and don'ts: we need books, time, and silence. Thou shalt not is soon forgotten, but Once upon a time lasts forever."
— Philip Pullman

201

"I want to be in a relationship where you telling me you love me is just a ceremonious validation of what you already show me."
— Steve Maraboli

202

"I've been fighting to be who I am all my life. What's the point of being who I am, if I can't have the person who was worth all the fighting for?"
— Stephanie Lennox

203

"The grand essentials to happiness in this life are something to do, something to love, and something to hope for."
— George Washington Burnap

204

"In life, finding a voice is speaking and living the truth. Each of you is an original. Each of you has a distinctive voice. When you find it, your story will be told. You will be heard."
— John Grisham

205

"I pray because I can't help myself. I pray because I'm helpless. I pray because the need flows out of me all the time- waking and sleeping. It doesn't change God- it changes me."
— William Nicholson

206

"Do no harm and leave the world a better place than you found it."
— Patricia Cornwell

207

"However many holy words you read, however many you speak, what good will they do you if you do not act on upon them?"
— Gautama Buddha

208

"I figured something out. The future is unpredictable."
— John Green

209

"Others have seen what is and asked why. I have seen what could be and asked why not. "
— Pablo Picasso

210

"Ask for what you want and be prepared to get it!"
— Maya Angelou

211

"I must be a mermaid, Rango. I have no fear of depths and a great fear of shallow living."
— Anaïs Nin

212

"Shoot for the moon. Even if you miss, you'll land among the stars."
— Norman Vincent Peale

213

"Whatever you can do or dream you can, begin it.
Boldness has genius, power and magic in it!"
— John Anster

214

"You can't wait for inspiration. You have to go after it with a club."

— Jack London

215

"Atticus, he was real nice."
"Most people are, Scout, when you finally see them."

— Harper Lee

216

"Incredible change happens in your life when you decide to take control of what you do have power over instead of craving control over what you don't."

— Steve Maraboli

217

"Be steady and well-ordered in your life so that you can be fierce and original in your work."
— Gustave Flaubert

218

"Only people who are capable of loving strongly can also suffer great sorrow, but this same necessity of loving serves to counteract their grief and heals them."
— Leo Tolstoy

219

"The question is not what you look at, but what you see."
— Henry David Thoreau

220

"I sought to hear the voice of God and climbed the topmost steeple, but God declared: "Go down again - I dwell among the people."
— John Henry Newman

221

"The starting point of all achievement is DESIRE. Keep this constantly in mind. Weak desire brings weak results, just as a small fire makes a small amount of heat."
— Napoleon Hill

222

"I am not afraid of storms, for I am learning how to sail my ship."
— Louisa May Alcott

223

"All thinking men are atheists."
— Ernest Hemingway

224

"I've known people that the world has thrown everything at to discourage them...to break their spirit. And yet something about them retains a dignity. They face life and don't ask quarters."
— Horton Foote

225

"A man who dares to waste one hour of time has not discovered the value of life."
— Charles Darwin

229
"I have never met a man so ignorant that I couldn't learn something from him."
— Galileo Galilei

230
"Keep your face always toward the sunshine - and shadows will fall behind you."
— Walt Whitman

231
"My only advice is to stay aware, listen carefully, and yell for help if you need it."
— Judy Blume

226

"There is nothing more dreadful than the habit of doubt. Doubt separates people. It is a poison that disintegrates friendships and breaks up pleasant relations. It is a thorn that irritates and hurts; it is a sword that kills."
— Gautama Buddha

227

"I am a part of all that I have met."
— Alfred Tennyson

228

"If you don't go after what you want, you'll never have it. If you don't ask, the answer is always no. If you don't step forward, you're always in the same place."
— Nora Roberts

232

"We never know the quality of someone else's life, though we seldom resist the temptation to assume and pass judgement."
— Tami Hoag

233

"The unhappiest people in this world, are those who care the most about what other people think."
— C. JoyBell C.

234

"Courage isn't having the strength to go on - it is going on when you don't have strength."
— Napoléon Bonaparte

235

"If you want to be happy, be."
— Leo Tolstoy

236

"I just want you to know that you're very special… and the only reason I'm telling you is that I don't know if anyone else ever has."
— Stephen Chbosky

237

"A concept is a brick. It can be used to build a courthouse of reason. Or it can be thrown through the window."
— Gilles Deleuze

238

"If we have no peace, it is
because we have forgotten that
we belong to each other."
— Mother Teresa

239

"The desire to reach for the stars
is ambitious. The desire to reach
hearts is wise."
— Maya Angelou

240

"No matter how plain a woman may
be, if truth and honesty are written
across her face, she will be beautiful."
— Eleanor Roosevelt

241

"Stepping onto a brand-new path is difficult, but not more difficult than remaining in a situation, which is not nurturing to the whole woman."
— Maya Angelou

242

"No matter how plain a woman may be, if truth and honesty are written across her face, she will be beautiful."
— Eleanor Roosevelt

243

"Romance is the glamour which turns the dust of everyday life into a golden haze. "
— Elinor Glyn

244
"Earth provides enough to satisfy every man's needs, but not every man's greed."
— Mahatma Gandhi

245
"No matter how your heart is grieving, if you keep on believing, the dreams that you wish will come true."
— Walt Disney Company

246
"The only thing standing between you and your goal is the bullshit story you keep telling yourself as to why you can't achieve it."
— Jordan Belfort

247

"Two roads diverged in a wood, and I -
I took the one less traveled by,
And that has made all the difference."
— Robert Frost

248

"The real heroes anyway aren't the
people doing things; the real heroes
are the people NOTICING things,
paying attention."
— John Green

249

"Tomorrow will be better."
"But what if it's not?" I asked.
"Then you say it again tomorrow.
Because it might be. You never know,
right? At some point, tomorrow will
be better."
— Morgan Matson

250

"Imagination is everything. It is the preview of life's coming attractions."
— Albert Einstein

251

"You might as well answer the door, my child,
the truth is furiously knocking."
— Lucille Clifton

252

If you make a mistake and do not correct it, this is called a mistake."
— Confucius

253
"Just because you can doesn't mean you should."
— Sherrilyn Kenyon

254
"Everything can be taken from a man but one thing: the last of the human freedoms—to choose one's attitude in any given set of circumstances, to choose one's own way."
— Viktor E. Frankl

255
"We are flawed creatures, all of us. Some of us think that means we should fix our flaws. But get rid of my flaws and there would be no one left."
— Sarah Vowell

256
"No matter what happens, or how bad it seems today, life does go on, and it will be better tomorrow."
— Maya Angelou

257
"It's hard to beat a person who never gives up."
— Babe Ruth

258
"Don't let the bastards grind you down."
— Margaret Atwood

259

"It was only a sunny smile, and little it cost in the giving, but like morning light it scattered the night and made the day worth living."
— F. Scott Fitzgerald

260

"Write it on your heart that every day is the best day in the year."
— Ralph Waldo Emerson

261

"I am not a teacher, but an awakener."
— Robert Frost

262

"True love is not so much a matter of romance as it is a matter of anxious concern for the well-being of one's companion."
— Gordon B. Hinckley

263

"why are trying so hard to fit in, when you're born to stand out"
— Oliver James

264

"Have courage for the great sorrows of life and patience for the small ones; and when you have laboriously accomplished your daily task, go to sleep in peace. God is awake."
— Victor Hugo

265

"The best thing to hold onto in
life is each other."
— Audrey Hepburn

266

"Because paper has more
patience than people. "
— Anne Frank

267

"Men are from Earth, women are
from Earth. Deal with it."
— George Carlin

268

"Sometimes God allows what he hates to accomplish what he loves."
— Joni Eareckson Tada

269

"Well, we all make mistakes, dear, so just put it behind you. We should regret our mistakes and learn from them, but never carry them forward into the future with us."
— L.M. Montgomery

270

"Sometimes life knocks you on your ass... get up, get up, get up!!! Happiness is not the absence of problems, it's the ability to deal with them."
— Steve Maraboli

271

"To love and win is the best thing.
To love and lose, the next best."
— William Makepeace Thackeray

272

"We don't make mistakes, just
happy little accidents."
— Bob Ross

273

"Happiness is not the absence of
problems, it's the ability to deal
with them."
— Steve Maraboli

274
"Where there is ruin, there is hope for a treasure."
— Jalaluddin Rumi

275
"The heart is the toughest part of the body.
Tenderness is in the hands."
— Carolyn Forché

276
"Not being heard is no reason for silence."
— Victor Hugo

277
"Hearts are breakable," Isabelle said.
"And I think even when you heal,
you're never what you were before"."
— Cassandra Clare

278
"Because,' she said, 'when you're
scared but you still do it anyway,
that's brave."
— Neil Gaiman

279
"Spoon feeding in the long run
teaches us nothing but the
shape of the spoon."
— E.M. Forster

280

"When someone tells me "no," it doesn't mean I can't do it, it simply means I can't do it with them."
— Karen E. Quinones Miller

281

"The soul is healed by being with children."
— Fyodor Dostoyevsky

282

"There is a candle in your heart, ready to be kindled.
There is a void in your soul, ready to be filled.
You feel it, don't you?"
— Jalaluddin Rumi

283

"I want to sing like the birds sing, not worrying about who hears or what they think."
— Jalaluddin Rumi

284

"Shoot for the moon, even if you fail, you'll land among the stars"
— Cecelia Ahern

285

"When I let go of what I am, I become what I might be."
— Lao Tzu

286

"God allows us to experience the low points of life in order to teach us lessons that we could learn in no other way."
— C.S. Lewis

287

"I have drunken deep of joy, And I will taste no other wine tonight."
— Percy Bysshe Shelley

288

"I never want to change so much that people can't recognize me."
— Taylor Swift

289

"For me, I am driven by two main philosophies: know more today about the world than I knew yesterday and lessen the suffering of others. You'd be surprised how far that gets you."
— Neil deGrasse Tyson

290

"I must be willing to give up what I am in order to become what I will be."
— Albert Einstein

291

"The reason birds can fly and we can't is simply because they have perfect faith, for to have faith is to have wings."
— J.M. Barrie

292
"Life sucks, and then you die..."
— Stephenie Meyer

293
"In the name of God, stop a
moment, cease your work, look
around you."
— Leo Tolstoy

294
"You'll never find a rainbow if
you're looking down"
— Charlie Chaplin

295

"I never saw a wild thing sorry for itself"
— D.H. Lawrence

296

"Death is no more than passing from one room into another. But there's a difference for me, you know. Because in that other room I shall be able to see."
— Helen Keller

297

"You only need one man to love you. But him to love you free like a wildfire, crazy like the moon, always like tomorrow, sudden like an inhale and overcoming like the tides. Only one man and all of this."
— C. JoyBell C.

298

"He that can have patience can have what he will."
— Benjamin Franklin

299

"Above all else, guard your heart for it affects everything else you do."
— Anonymous

300

"Do stuff. be clenched, curious. Not waiting for inspiration's shove or society's kiss on your forehead. Pay attention. It's all about paying attention. attention is vitality. It connects you with others. It makes you eager. stay eager."
— Susan Sontag

301

"Wanting to be someone else is a waste of who you are"
— Kurt Cobain

302

"Don't be afraid of enemies who attack you. Be afraid of the friends who flatter you."
— Dale Carnegie

303

"Last night I lost the world, and gained the universe."
— C. JoyBell C.

304

"Swords can win territories but not hearts, forces can bend heads but not minds."
— Mirza Tahir Ahmad

305

"Everybody is special. Everybody. Everybody is a hero, a lover, a fool, a villain. Everybody. Everybody has their story to tell."
— Alan Moore

306

"The biggest adventure you can ever take is to live the life of your dreams."
— Oprah Winfrey

307

"No one really knows why they are alive until they know what they'd die for."
— Martin Luther King Jr.

308

"Risks must be taken because the greatest hazard in life is to risk nothing."
— Leo Buscaglia

309

"The only person who can pull me down is myself, and I'm not going to let myself pull me down anymore."
— C. JoyBell C.

310

"Death is not the greatest loss in life. The greatest loss is what dies inside while still alive. Never surrender."
— Tupac Shakur

311

"The higher we soar the smaller we appear to those who cannot fly."
— Friedrich Nietzsche

312

"Change the way you look at things and the things you look at change."
— Wayne W. Dyer

313

"I live my life in widening circles
that reach out across the world."
— Rainer Maria Rilke

314

"Aim higher in case you fall short."
— Suzanne Collins

315

"A Penny Saved is a Penny
Earned"
— Benjamin Franklin

316

"In the end you should always do the right thing even if it's hard."
— Nicholas Sparks

317

"The damage was permanent; there would always be scars. But even the angriest scars faded over time until it was difficult to see them written on the skin at all, and the only thing that remained was the memory of how painful it had been."
— Jodi Picoult

318

"We travel, some of us forever, to seek other states, other lives, other souls."
— Anaïs Nin

319

"Do not seek the because - in love there is no because, no reason, no explanation, no solutions."
— Anaïs Nin

320

"When all is said and done, more is said than done."
— Lou Holtz

321

"If you want to be happy, do not dwell in the past, do not worry about the future, focus on living fully in the present."
— Roy T. Bennett

322

"Many of life's failures are people who did not realize how close they were to success when they gave up."
— Thomas A. Edison

323

"Our wounds are often the openings into the best and most beautiful part of us."
— David Richo

324

"Make the most of yourself....for that is all there is of you."
— Ralph Waldo Emerson

325

"The mediocre teacher tells. The good teacher explains. The superior teacher demonstrates. The great teacher inspires."
— William Arthur Ward

326

"The best things in life make you sweaty."
— Edgar Allan Poe

327

"Believe you can and you're halfway there."
— Theodore Roosevelt

328
"We meet no ordinary people in
our lives."
— C.S. Lewis

329
"When in a relationship, a real
man doesn't make his woman
jealous of others, he makes
others jealous of his woman."
— Steve Maraboli

330
"If your feet are firmly planted
on the ground you'll never be
able to dance."
— Iris Johansen

331

"For like a shaft, clear and cold, the thought pierced him that in the end the Shadow was only a small and passing thing: there was light and high beauty for ever beyond its reach."
— J.R.R. Tolkien

332

"The windows of my soul I throw Wide open to the sun."
— John Greenleaf Whittier

333

"Aerodynamically, the bumble bee shouldn't be able to fly, but the bumble bee doesn't know it so it goes on flying anyway."
— Mary Kay Ash

334

"There's so much to be grateful for, words are poor things."
— Marilynne Robinson

335

"No one loses anyone, because no one owns anyone. That is the true experience of freedom: having the most important thing in the world without owning it"
— Paulo Coelho

336

"Every man is a damn fool for at least five minutes every day; wisdom consists in not exceeding the limit."
— Elbert Hubbard

337
"Music melts all the separate parts of our bodies together."
— Anaïs Nin

338
"I like nonsense, it wakes up the brain cells. Fantasy is a necessary ingredient in living, It's a way of looking at life through the wrong end of a telescope. Which is what I do, And that enables you to laugh at life's realities."
— Dr. Seuss

339
"Just be yourself, there is no one better."
— Taylor Swift

340
"I'd rather learn from one bird
how to sing
than teach ten thousand stars
how not to dance"
— E.E. Cummings

341

"All the effort in the world won't
matter if you're not inspired."
— Chuck Palahniuk

342
"So it's true, when all is said and
done, grief is the price we pay
for love."
— E.A. Bucchianeri

343

"There are two ways to reach me: by way of kisses or by way of the imagination. But there is a hierarchy: the kisses alone don't work."
— Anaïs Nin

344

"There is the great lesson of 'Beauty and the Beast,' that a thing must be loved before it is lovable."
— G.K. Chesterton

345

"Scar tissue is stronger than regular tissue. Realize the strength, move on."
— Henry Rollins

346

"Nothing great was ever
achieved without enthusiasm."
— Ralph Waldo Emerson

347

"Dream as if you will live forever;
Live as if you will die today."
— James Dean

348

"She was free in her wildness.
She was a wanderess, a drop of
free water. She belonged to no
man and to no city"
— Roman Payne

349

"There is no dishonor in losing the race. There is only dishonor in not racing because you are afraid to lose."
— Garth Stein

350

"Fiction is art and art is the triumph over chaos… to celebrate a world that lies spread out around us like a bewildering and stupendous dream."
— John Cheever

351

"I have been and still am a seeker, but I have ceased to question stars and books; I have begun to listen to the teaching my blood whispers to me."
— Hermann Hesse

352

"A man with outward courage
dares to die; a man with inner
courage dares to live."
— Lao Tzu

353

"Travel far enough, you meet
yourself."
— David Mitchell

354

"We are products of our past, but we
don't have to be prisoners of it."
— Rick Warren

355

"Be more concerned with your character than your reputation, because your character is what you really are, while your reputation is merely what others think you are."
— John Wooden

356

"Without fear there cannot be courage."
— Christopher Paolini

357

"I shall look at you out of the corner of my eye, and you will say nothing. Words are the source of misunderstandings."
— Antoine de Saint-Exupéry

358

"Always dream and shoot higher than you know you can do. Do not bother just to be better than your contemporaries or predecessors. Try to be better than yourself."
— William Faulkner

359

"I never made one of my discoveries through the process of rational thinking"
— Albert Einstein

360

"Home is the place where, when you have to go there, they have to take you in."
— Robert Frost

361

"If you are lazy, and accept your lot, you may live in it. If you are willing to work, you can write your name anywhere you choose."
— Gene Stratton-Porter

362

"I may not always be with you
But when we're far apart
Remember you will be with me
Right inside my heart"
— Marc Wambolt

363

"Too often we underestimate the power of a touch, a smile, a kind word, a listening ear, an honest compliment, or the smallest act of caring, all of which have the potential to turn a life around."
— Leo Buscaglia

364
"Those who look for the bad in people
will surely find it."
— Abraham Lincoln

365
"What a large volume of adventures
may be grasped within the span of his
little life by him who interests his
heart in everything."
— Laurence Sterne

366
"We either make ourselves miserable,
or we make ourselves strong. The
amount of work is the same."
— Carlos Castaneda

—

Made in the USA
Coppell, TX
03 March 2022

74358241R00069